My dearest friends

and the heights of b~~eauty while rolling~~ with me through all of the mundane that exists between the two. Deep friendship requires risk, pain, forgiveness, and return. It's there in the festive celebration and by the graveside of loss. Jesus is our greatest example of friendship as he opened his arms wide, moved toward us in our brokenness, and chose us! Jesus walks in friendship while speaking truth into our hearts, healing us all along the way. This gospel gives us news eyes and a new way to view and live in friendship and this book will give you a view into the beauty of the gospel and how it really does transform friendship.

CHARLIE HALL,
Worship Arts & Liturgy Pastor
Frontline church Oklahoma City

Here is a spiritually uplifting study of friendship, a Gospel theme too much neglected in theology today. A worthy guide for all friends of the Savior on the pilgrimage of faith.

TIMOTHY GEORGE,
Founding Dean of Beeson Divinity School of Samford
University and General editor of the Reformation
Commentary on Scripture.

A happy blend of biblical principles, personal insight, experience, and engaging devotional style, Holland's Biblical Friendship is a fresh and timely contribution on the subject from a Christian perspective. I'll be a better friend for having read it.

DAVID L. ALLEN,
Dean of the School of Theology Professor of Preaching,
Southwestern Baptist Theological

Paul is often viewed as the model missionary, pastor or prayer warrior! He is not generally known for his friendships. Yet there is so much to glean from this rich aspect of his life. Holland is a good and helpful guide in taking us into Paul's friendships and in doing so exhorts us in our own, both to enjoy the gift they are and the good they do in helping us grow in conformity to Christ.

STEVE TIMMIS,
Founder of The Crowded House, a Director of Acts 29 Europe, Author of Gospel-Centered Leadership and co-author of Total Church and Everyday Church, & board-member of the Biblical Counseling Coalition.

Friendship—with God, with spouses, with countless other people—is one of life's great blessings. It was also important for many people known to us from Scripture, such as the Apostle Paul. May Adam Holland's book do for a new genera-tion of Christians what William Pierson Barker's Saints in Aprons and Overalls: Friends of Paul did for an earlier gen-eration.

JOHN T FITZGERALD,
Professor of New Testament and Early Christianity, University of Notre Dame

The apostle Paul has often been depicted as a missionary loner who was abrasive and who had a hard time making and keeping friends (he even had a falling out with Barnabas over John Mark!). But this caricature could not be farther from the truth. A careful reading of Paul's letters shows clearly that Paul had many friends, and that he truly loved and needed others. This wonderful and encouraging little book intro-duces us to several of Paul's friends, and shows us how vital Paul's friends were for his life and ministry. More impor-tantly, it teaches us through biblical examples what Christian friendship looks like, and of the importance of having friends and of being a friend to others. It reminds us of the risks of friendship, the reality of broken friendships and the joy of friendships restored (even with John Mark!). But it also dem-onstrates clearly how important Christian friendships are for living the Christian life and serving God faithfully. Kingdom-minded friends encourage us, help us carry our burdens, min-ister spiritual healing to us, forgive us, and love us with the love that comes only from the triune God who has existed eternally in loving fellowship. This book will encourage you to seek and build the kind of friendships that Paul had, and so will make your life and service for Christ richer, fuller and more faithful.

DR. BILL BARCLEY,
Senior Pastor, Sovereign Grace Presbyterian Church,
Adjunct Professor, Reformed Theological Seminary

Few things are more wonderful than a true friendship, yet our thoughts about friendship are often thin and our practices weak. Adam Holland has written a bright, accessible, Christ-centered account of true friendship that gives every reader an opportunity to deepen their ideas and habits. The core of the book is a unique series of studies in Paul's friendships. Linked with chapters on friendship, the gospel, and the kingdom, this book is ideal for discipleship studies.

DR. DAN DORIANI
Vice President of Strategic Academic Projects and Professor of Theology at Covenant Theological Seminary

In a world like ours, "friends" are easy to make on social media, but real friends can be hard to come by. In this book Adam Holland explores a set of ancient characters, bound together through their friendship with the apostle Paul. Each of these comes to life in the lively pen portraits Adam presents, depicting their lives and ours as closer than we might imagine. He deals with the difficulties as well as the joys of real friendship, and grounds all these connections not just in Paul's friendship they shared, but in friendship with Jesus that all of us share. This book sheds light on friends, on these New Testament figures and their friend Paul, and on a neglected gift of the Gospel.

ANDREW MCGOWAN
Dean and President of Berkeley Divinity School and McFaddin Professor of Anglican Studies and Pastoral Theology at Yale University

VERITAS PRESS

Veritas Press exists to glorify God by creating truth-centered resources for human flourishing.

Other Veritas Press resources:

Date Different: A Short (but real) Conversation on Dating, Sex, and Marriage for Teenagers (and their parents)

Follow VP on Twitter @Veritas_Press

Purchase at TheVeritasNetwork.org

FRIENDSHIP REDEEMED

How the Gospel Changes
Friendships to Something Greater

ADAM HOLLAND

VERITAS PRESS
2015

To the Henrichs, Hoovers, Pullens, and Stooksburys.

You all have played a key role in shaping my understanding of friendship. It has been through friendships with you all that I have learned what the gospel on the ground level looks like.

There is nothing on this earth more to be prized than true friendship. — Thomas Aquinas (1225–1274)

TABLE OF CONTENT

1
THE GOSPEL CHANGES EVERYTHING

"No longer do I call you slaves, for the slave does not know what his master is doing; but I have called you friends" — Jesus

I was riding down the road without a care in the world. The windows were down in my grandfather's old beat-up F-150. Merle and Garth were cranked up loud on the radio. The music wasn't loud so as to overpower the drivers beside us, but was loud so that we could hear it over the noise of the engine and wind. If I close my eyes even now, I can still feel the summer breeze blowing over my arm as it hung out the window. These rides were filled with many laughs and smiles. Somehow our conversations always evolved into plans of fishing in the near future. We were both enjoying the journey and somehow the melancholy of a weekly trash dump visit managed to blow away with the wind over my arm.

TIME SPENT WITH A FRIEND

Time spent with a friend has the unique ability to pass time and even make the most mundane moments enjoyable. Not only does time spent with friends give quality to time, but it also creates lasting memories. I am often baffled when I meet or hear about people who never leave their homes and deny themselves of friendships and memories such as these.

I can't recall a single night in my life where sitting at home and watching television was truly life transforming. On the other hand, there are many conversations and times of fellowship that I can point to as being turning points in my life. Sometimes, the weightiness of a conversation with a dear friend can hold down the minute hand on a clock. I glance at my watch only to realize that I needed to be somewhere fifteen minutes earlier. After the panic of getting out the door fades away, I am reminded how much I enjoyed my time with this particular person. Why don't all friendships contain these qualities?

THE TASTE OF TRUE FRIENDSHIP

Deep friendship and true intimacy within a friendship give testimony to a heavenly reality. Great friendships have the aroma and taste of another world. This is similar to how Edmund, in C.S. Lewis's, *Chronicles of Narnia*, tastes the magical dessert "Turkish Delight" in the land of Narnia.

The taste of this dessert makes him desire to return to Narnia, so he can taste of its wonder once more. Friendship is similar to this. Once a person experiences true friendship, he longs to taste of its beauty once again. This type of friendship causes its participants to yearn for their heavenly home. The only way for something like this to exist is if it were created by and for something greater.

Mankind was created in the image of the triune God. We were created to live in harmony or perfect unity with one another. Our relationships with one another are and were to be a reflection of the relationship that the Godhead has had within itself throughout eternity. The Christian is called to bring these heavenly realities down to earth. When an unbeliever sees a Christian friendship, he gets to see a small glimpse of what the world looks like when it is ruled by Christ. They get to see a glimpse of what it looks like when the Shalom, or peace of God, has been restored in the world. What, then, caused our relationships to go haywire and stop displaying heavenly realities?

THE REALITIES OF SIN IN FRIENDSHIP

Once sin entered into the world it not only separated us from God, but it also separated us from one another. Sin distorted and hid that image. That which was intended to be plain within our relationships can now only be seen through distorted glasses. Our unity and harmony now look more like a carnival mirror maze than they do a reflection of God. The disobedience that took place in the Garden of Eden continues its destruction in our relationships today just as it did then.

Once sin entered into the world, Adam and Eve hid from one another in shame. The shame and hiddenness that resulted from the Fall continues to carry over into many of our relationships today. One of the biggest killers of authenticity and true communion within relationships is our tendency to hide and hold ourselves back from one another. We hurt and struggle, but we keep it to ourselves rather than reach out to those who love us.

We struggle with trust and vulnerability, because we fear getting hurt within a relationship. Thus we hide, and no one ever truly gets to know who we really are. We put up walls and pray that no one sees past the fig leaves we have sown to hide ourselves from others. Is there any hope that

our relationships can fulfill their intended purpose?

THE HOPE FOR FRIENDSHIP

Our hope for transformation within our relationships comes from the same hope which Adam
and Eve received in Genesis 3:15. In Genesis 3:15,
right after the Fall of man, God promised Eve that
her seed would one day crush the head of the
serpent. This promise, and the hope of its fulfill-
ment, became a major theme throughout the Old
Testament.[1]

Ultimately this passage would find its fulfill-
ment in Jesus on the cross. At Golgotha, the place
of the skull or head (Matt. 27:33), Jesus crushes
the head of the serpent and sets his people free.
The New Testament writers saw what Jesus did
on the cross as the event of all events. It is literally the event that changes all of history.

If you are a parent and can remember your
life pre-children (like a parent really has time for
this type of thinking), every so often you may

---

1 In the very next chapter, there is enmity between Cain and Abel (e.g.,
the seed of the serpent and the seed of promise). Cain kills Abel and it
seems like the serpent has triumphed, but God then provides Seth. In John
8, Jesus ties how Cain murdered Abel to an action of the serpent. The
story of the Exodus is later described as God crushing the head of the
serpent (Ps. 74:14; Isaiah 27:1). In the story of David and Goliath, David
(the Shepherd-King) cuts the head off of Goliath. Goliath dresses himself
as a serpent (1 Sam. 17:5). It is through Goliath's head crushing that Israel
is set free. For further reading on this head crushing motif read:
http://jimhamilton.info/wp-content/uploads/2008/04/hamilton_sbjt_10-2.p
df

think, "What did I do with all my free time before I had children?" Having children has the unique ability to zap up all of your free time. Having young children also forces a parent to rethink their entire schedule, "What must I do, re-arrange, and change in order to get everything that I need done for the day?"

Before having children, you can literally do anything you want, whenever you want. The reason I bring this up is not to scare all the married couples out there who are considering having children, but to give a concrete example of an event that changes everything about your life.

For those who lived during the time of Jesus, his death and resurrection far outweighed the life-altering impact of having children. Jesus' resurrection literally meant the end of the physical temple, a place that played a central role in a Jew's everyday life. This event meant the end of the sacrificial system, a system that also was a normative part of the Jewish life. This event meant that those who put their faith in the finished work of Jesus would have to learn to live differently. These early Christians would have to learn what it meant to live on the other side of the cross. The cross wasn't simply a life-altering event for those living in the early church, it is also a life-altering event for the modern person who puts their faith and trust in Jesus as Lord.

FRIENDSHIP REDEEMED

You may be thinking, "Why do I need to learn to how to live on this side the cross? I have been raised in church my entire life. I used to destroy other kids in bible drill." My response to this sort of thinking is simple: that which you and I may believe to be natural and assumed, may actually be far from the true difficulty of the task. Living in light of the cross calls for a person to learn a new way to live life. When a person puts their faith in Jesus Christ, he must learn to think Christianly. Jesus, when explaining to Nicodemus what a person must do in order to enter the kingdom of God, explains that "he must be born again." Paul, writing to the Corinthians, says, "If anyone is in Christ, he is a new creation."

As Christians, we are learning to live life as a part of the new humanity. Peter Leithart, in his book *Against Christianity*, is helpful in explaining how living as a part of this new humanity is more than just adding a new list of "do this and don't do that" to one's life. Leithart says,

> Conversion does not simply install a new 're-ligious' program over the existing operating system. Christian community, by the same token, is not an extra 'religious' layer on so-cial life. The church is not a club for religious people. The church is a way of living together

before God, a new way of being human together.[2]

Living in this new humanity calls for far more than just adding or taking away a few things from your life. Fixing our relationships with one another is not going to be resolved by a 10-step program or adding just a couple things. Living in this new humanity calls for a person to put on a new pair of glasses, through which he will look and see the world.

It is as radical as when a man puts his faith in Christ. He then receives the Spirit, returns to the carnival mirror maze mentioned earlier with a sledge hammer, and breaks every piece of glass in the building. After Jesus' resurrection, Jesus' disciples were walking along the road to Emmaus. Jesus, then, draws near to them and begins to have a conversation with them. Luke says that at the time Jesus "blinded their eyes, so that they would not recognize him."

Jesus begins in Genesis and goes through the entire Old Testament and shows the disciples how all of scripture looked forward to him." That would've been one incredible conversation to sit in on! For the disciples, Jesus' resurrection didn't mean adding on something new to their already existing belief structure. Jesus' resurrection meant re-interpreting everything they ever knew. Just as the disciples must learn what it meant to

---

2 Peter Leithart, *Against Christianity* (Moscow, Id: Canon Press. 2003), 16.

live in light of the cross, we too must learn this reality. If living in this new humanity calls for that significant of a life change, where can one go to see a model of what this looks like?

If we truly want to fix our relationships and have our relationships fulfill their intended purpose, we need an example in which to look. The famous agrarian and short story writer Wendell Berry once said, "It is not from ourselves that we learn to be better than we are." We need an example to demonstrate to us how to live. Imagine that you never saw a football game in your entire life. It would not be likely that you would ever become a football player. Imagine now that you had Peyton Manning come teach you about football and train you how to play the game. The chances of you growing in your knowledge and ability to play football would increase dramatically.[3]

One of the best places one can go to see what it looks like to live Christianly is the Apostle Paul. Paul models what it looks like when the gospel takes root in a person's life and friendships. One of the best places to see how the gospel transformed Paul's understanding of friendship is in Colossians 4.

---

3 Wendell Berry, *The Long-Legged House* (San Diego, Ca: Harcourt, Brace & World Publishing, 2004), 210.

2
TYCHICUS

I walked outside and a winter breeze hit my skin like a Mack truck. It was pitch black, and the majority of the world was still nestled into their warm comfy beds. The sun had even determined that it was too early to get out bed. What type of friend would talk me into missing sleep in the heart of winter for this? These circumstances caused me to question the validity and future of our relationship. When I finally met up with him, the moon was still in full bloom in the night sky. I stepped out of my car only to hear the sound of crickets and a river stream. The image of the fog hovering over the water was reminiscent to that of a Bob Ross painting. We spent the rest of the morning fishing and enjoying life. We spent more time talking about life than we actually did catching fish. The day ended up being an incredible day. Some may think that our fishing results depreciated the value of the trip.

You couldn't put a price on that time we spent together. The river that morning became the guy's version of "beauty shop talk," but without the gossip. Our time was spent enjoying the beauty of God's creation and having conversations about what the Lord was doing in our lives. This fishing trip would've never taken place if it weren't for this dear friend encouraging me and tormenting me to go. Relationships such as these require love and time spent together.

VERTICAL AND HORIZONTAL

In the Garden of Eden, God spoke to Adam and Eve and told them not to eat from the "Tree of Knowledge of Good and Evil." As soon as the serpent is introduced, he attacks and convinces Adam and Eve to question God and His word. The serpent begins his attack by saying, "Did God really say?" The serpent begins with skepticism. The serpent continues his attack by sowing seeds of doubt, by questioning the character of God and telling Eve, "You will not surely die if you touch it. For God knows that when you eat of it your eyes will be opened, and you will be like God, knowing good and evil."

What began as questioning the trustworthiness of God's Word, progressed to questioning the character of God. Adam and Eve were given a command, and they chose to put their reason above the reason of God. The serpent's goal was to convince the couple to think and reason outside of God's word. Rather than remain faithful to the Lord, Adam and Eve rejected God's word as their final authority. This rebellion not only caused destruction within man's relationship with God, but it also caused destruction within man's relationship with one another. Dietrich Bonhoeffer explains how both fellowship and love of others begins with our relationship with God. He explains this by saying,

> The first service that one owes to others in fellowship consists in listening to them. Just as love to God begins with listening to His word, so the beginning of love for brethren is learning to listen to them.[4]

Man learns how to interact with one another through how they interact and relate to God. Once man sins by refusing to listen and obey the word of God, it then impacts man's relationship with one another. Adam then blames Eve and Eve the serpent. Because of their unfaithfulness, Adam and Eve are then kicked out of God's presence and land.

When our vertical relationship with the Lord is not right, it has ramifications into our horizontal relationships with one another. Where do I get this concept from? You may be thinking I have unbelieving friends who have great relationships with other nonbelievers. Why would quality rela-

---

4 Dietrich Bonhoeffer, *Life Together: The Classic Exploration of Christian in Community,* trans. John W. Doberstein (New York, NY: Harper and Row Publishing Company, 1954), 97.

tionships with one another necessitate a relationship with the Lord? The book of Proverbs is helpful in explaining this.

EVERYTHING FLOWS FROM GOD

The book of Proverbs is wisdom for living. A great deal of the book of Proverbs is written about how to live well with others. It is interesting that Solomon says, "The fear of the Lord is the beginning of all wisdom (Prov. 9:10)." Our ability to live well and have relationships with others begins, and has as its constant antecedent, in man's relationship with the Lord. This is not something that you can abandon and still expect your friendships to flourish. It is when humanity tried and tries to live life and experience life's joys apart from the Lord that things go sour. As the reader leaves the Garden of Eden and continues through the rest of the Old Testament narrative, man continues to live life without acknowledging his creator.

Over and over again, God's people are called to faithfulness and obedience to YHWH, but they fail. God delivers Israel out of the slavery to Egypt, yet while they are in the wilderness, they constantly want to return because they thought they were better off in slavery. Israel finally arrives at the promise land and God delivers His law to them through Moses. After hearing the law, Israel responds to the Lord, saying, "All that the LORD has spoken we will do, and we will be obedient." Once again like Adam, Israel disobeys the Lord. They are unfaithful to their bridegroom. They choose other foreign gods over him. As a result of their unfaithfulness, like Adam and Eve, God kicks Israel out of the land. Once again, man's unfaithfulness to God will mirror itself in their relationships with the rest of humanity.

One of the commandments from the law, which God gave to Moses, called for Israel to "not bear false witness (Ex. 20:16)." The writer of Proverbs reiterates this by saying, "Lying lips are an abomination to the Lord" (Prov. 12:12). With sin came distrust and dishonesty throughout mankind. The writer of Proverbs would later say, "A dishonest man spreads strife, and a whisperer separates close friends" (Prov. 16:28). It was a lack of trust that separated man from God, and it is likewise the absence of trust and truth that further divides our relationships. The reason many people do not share their struggles and hurts with their friends is because they struggle with trust. Mankind has proven to them that a good friend is hard to find. Is there any hope for recovery for this loss of faithfulness, truth, and honesty?

FRIENDSHIP MADE NEW IN CHRIST

When you come to the New Testament, Jesus lives the life mankind could not live. Jesus, like Israel, is tempted in the wilderness for 40-days, but he remains faithful. Jesus goes up on the mountain similar to how Moses goes up on the mountain and receives the law. Jesus then explains the law and calls for an even greater righteousness than that for which the law from Sinai called. God said through Moses, "Do not murder." Jesus says, "If you have hated in your heart, you have committed murder." The law also says, "Do not commit adultery." Jesus takes that a step further and says, "If you have lusted in your heart, you have committed adultery." The life which man failed to live, Christ comes, lives, and demands an even greater righteousness than that which was given in the Law. Where the people of Israel complained and grumbled about the manna in the wilderness, Jesus comes and feeds the multitudes and offers them the Bread of Life. Where mankind constantly failed, grumbled, and did not offer worship to the Lord, Christ comes and perfectly obeys the Lord and willingly lays down his life.

By his death, mankind can now be reconciled to the Father. Christ's death makes reconciliation possible not only with God, but also with one another. If you have been made new in Christ Jesus, you are called to represent the King and his redemption to the rest of humanity. William Still, a famous Anglican minister, explains this concept this way, saying, "The word became flesh, and it must become flesh again in you."[5] The Christian is called to live in such a way that reflects the re-

---

5 William Still, *The Work of the Pastor* (Ross-shire, UK: Christian Focus Publications, 2010), 24.

ality that Jesus has defeated sin, and the Father is restoring all things under the reign of King Christ (Eph. 2:20-21). Because of what Christ has done there is hope for our friendships to restore truth, trust, and faithfulness. In Colossians 4, the Apostle Paul gives an example of a man who truly demonstrated the power of the gospel to transform. In this example, Paul describes his faithful friend Tychicus.

DEVELOPING FRIENDSHIPS OF TRUST

One aspect of the ministry of the Apostle Paul was to train the church to think Christianly. Remember, Paul was not just encouraging early believers to add a few things to their weekly routine. Paul wanted to train the Colossians how to live on the other side of the cross. The cross demands for the Christian to look at the world from an entire new pair of glasses. In the last chapter of his letter to the Colossian Church, Paul begins by mentioning his friend Tychicus. These stories give the reader a glimpse into how Paul viewed friendship. Who was Paul's friend Tychicus?

You have likely never heard of Tychicus. You won't find his name on any "Who's Who of Biblical Heroes" list. Even though most people have never heard his name, he played an important role in the life and ministry of the Apostle Paul. Similar to a good friend, he may not be famous in the world's eyes, but his value is far greater than anything fame could buy.

TYCHICUS

Tychicus was the type of friend that you could call in the middle of the night and he would come over to talk some sense into you. He would come over and help you work through your problems. Tychicus is the guy that you couldn't get rid of because he wouldn't give up on you that easily. Tychicus would correct you when correction was needed, but he would also be the guy that says the right thing when you were hurting.

Paul begins by describing Tychicus as a "beloved brother." This term "beloved" is used constantly throughout the New Testament to depict the love the Father has for Jesus (Matt. 3:17; 12:18; 17:5; Mark 1:11; 9:7; Luke 20:13). This would not be a term Paul would use flippantly. Paul's love toward Tychicus was a heavenly reality that was lived out here on earth. Their relationship may not have been a perfect reflection of heaven, but it certainly was a reflection nonetheless. Tychicus was a best friend to Paul. Paul wasn't simply exaggerating his relationship with this man. Paul wasn't trying to make Tychicus sound greater than he was. In fact, Paul brings up Tychicus' significance on several occasions. When Paul wrote to the church at Ephesus, he describes Tychicus as a "Beloved brother and faithful minister (Eph. 6:21)." Tychicus was the guy that encouraged others while they were in the midst of life's struggles. Paul tells the Colossians that he is sending Tychicus to them "for this very purpose, that you [The Colossians] may know how we are and that he may encourage your hearts."

WORDS OF ENCOURAGEMENT

Tychicus was sent to encourage the faint-hearted and encourage these believers to faithful ministry. In several places throughout the New Testament, the ministry of the Holy Spirit is described as that of "comforting," "strengthening," and "encouraging (John 15:16-7, 14:26-27; Acts 2:14, 9:31, 13:52)." Tychicus is called to go and demonstrate to these churches what it looks like to live a Spirit-filled life. All too often we equate a Spirit-filled life with Pentecostalism or charismatic gifts. Some run to, and others flee from, conversations about the Spirit because of these things. No matter what end of the spectrum you end up on in the conversation, everyone should be able to agree that a Spirit-filled life is one that is characterized by the fruits of the Spirit.[6] Tychicus' life was a Spirit-filled life. Tychicus's life could be characterized as one who brought heavenly realities down to earth. Tychicus had proven he could be trusted with anything.

Paul had a deep-seated trust for Tychicus. Paul sent Tychicus to the churches at Colossae, Crete, and Ephesus to update them on Paul's missionary journey. Paul trusted Tychicus to represent him to God's people. Just as a country would

---

6 The obvious would be a life characterized by those characteristics listed in Galatians 5:22-23. We should not neglect other 'fruits' of the Spirit such as "comforting"/ "strengthening" [cf., John 14:26], being a "helper" [cf., John 14:16], pointing a person to Christ [cf., John 15:25-26], and etc.

not take lightly selecting an ambassador to represent its nation to visiting countries, Paul likewise would've taken even more care in selecting an ambassador for God's kingdom. Early church tradition taught that Tychicus was one who carried many of Paul's letters to the churches. Tychicus was not a Second Temple mailman. Paul is entrusting this man with delivering the very Word of God to these congregations. If Tychicus had not been careful or trustworthy, you and I would not have several letters we have in our New Testament. Tychicus was a friend who could be trusted with the most important things in life. Not only was Tychicus trustworthy, but he also seemed to always know the right words to say.

CHOOSING THE RIGHT THING TO SAY

We have already discussed how Tychicus was an encourager. Someone who is gifted at encouragement has the ability to say the right thing at the right time. A good encourager knows exactly what to say in order to motivate you to move forward. Tychicus' ability to carefully choose the right words likely played into Paul's reasoning for choosing him to escort Onesimus back to his slave owner.

Onesimus, who we will examine in the next chapter, was a former slave who fled from his master. In Onesimus' pursuits of freedom, he was converted to Christ and met the Apostle Paul. Paul, then, sends Onesimus back to his slave owner with Tychicus. This is an extremely sensitive issue. Onesimus could very well be put to death for his actions. Paul knows this and because of this, he sends Onesimus with his other dear friend Tychicus. Paul sends Tychicus to urge Philemon (the slave owner) to spare Onesimus' life and also to urge him to set him free. Tychicus goes and pleads for a man's life, but also for his freedom from slavery.

DO YOU HAVE A FRIEND LIKE THAT?

Do you have a Tychicus in your life? Do you have friends that are like Tychicus? We all need friends like this. Everyone needs an encourager in his or her life. We need someone who will motivate us to faithfulness to the mission of God. We need someone who will bring hope into our lives when the world's waves crash down on us. Furthermore, we need the type of friend that knows the right thing to say at the right time. Christian friendship should be characterized by trustworthiness and honesty. Not only do we need friends like Tychicus in our lives, we also need to display these qualities to others. Christians are called to love one another (Jn. 13:34).Right before Paul mentions Tychicus he calls the Colossians to "bear with one another (Col 3:13)." Paul says Christians should be "devoted to one another (Rom. 12:10)." In that same letter he later says that we are to "build up one another (Rom. 14:19). This is not a checklist that you can check and then declare that you are a good friend. Paul is training these believers to live life in light of the cross.

This list is certainly not exhaustive. Paul gives us the example of Tychicus to show us what it looks like to live on the other side of the cross. Pray that the Spirit would manifest these attributes in your life and relationships. Go have coffee with a friend, open up your heart and life to them. Plan a fishing trip with a buddy. The fishing trip is only an excuse to get together and grow your relationship. May your relationships grow as big as the fish you claim to have caught. Finally, ask the Lord to bring you and turn you into a Tychicus, so that your relationships may grow in maturity and authenticity.

3
ONESIMUS

What began as a fun day spawned into an intense battle. We arrived before dinnertime, just in time to sit down and work it all out. We stared at one another across the table, our faces looked like a war-time battle was developing. I was waiting for Mel Gibson to burst on the scene and scream, "FREEDOM!" As time went on our emotions only intensified. Before any casualties had taken place, a sudden cease-fire was declared. My wife walked up to the checkerboard table and let my five-year-old daughter and I know that our dinner at Cracker Barrel had arrived. Once Mom came and raised the white flag our game had to end.

TIME SPENT WITH A GREAT FRIEND

I cherish games of checkers with my kids. What may look like a simple game with children to some, I see as a treasure trove of love waiting to be mined. My love for games exists outside of my children as well. I love to get together with friends and play cards. If I were honest the cards are just an excuse to get to spend time with my friends. It seems like I have a lot of things in life that are like that. Games are a great excuse to spend time with friends. As the game comes to an end, I am faced with the painful reality that this incredible time of fellowship must also come to an end. We all have friends where it hurts when we leave their presence. The Apostle Paul was no different than us; he too had wonderful friendships such as these.

A FRIEND LIKE ONESIMUS

We have already briefly discussed Onesimus. He was not your stereotypical friend. Onesimus had a somewhat unusual past, and he was a slave who converted to Christ. After his salvation, he became a ministry partner to Paul. Onesimus would be similar to a convict-to-Christ conversion story. Growing up, I would always hear people say, "I wish (Insert popular cultural figure's name) would convert to Christianity. If 'X' would convert, he would make a major impact for the name of Christ." I always found these comments ironic and comical.

We sometimes think that God only uses important people, or people with great backgrounds, to accomplish kingdom advancement, but most often in scripture God uses the unlikely, the little people, and makes them great. Francis

Schaeffer was accurate when he explained that there are "no little people" in the kingdom of God. Whether great or small, whether dramatic conversion story or not, all conversions tell the story of an amazing Lord. Onesimus' story is our story: a slave who has been set free and transformed by the gospel. His story is an incredible testimony to the fact that God can use anyone for His kingdom purposes.

THE GOSPEL GIVES VALUE TO THE VALUELESS

Do you feel insignificant? Maybe you have a bad past? If so, listen to the way Paul talks about his friend Onesimus, saying, "Formerly he was useless to you, but now he is indeed useful to you and to me (Phil 1:11)." The gospel transforms what the world sees as ordinary and useless and makes it into something great and beautiful. The world once saw this man as having no value, but now he has become a friend and ministry partner to Paul.

Paul describes his friend Onesimus in several different ways. Paul says that Onesimus has "served" him while he was in prison. Paul calls Onesimus "beloved," just as he did with Tychicus. Paul tells Philemon that by sending him Onesimus he is sending him "his very heart." Do you have a friend that is so close that when you depart it is as if part of yourself is walking out the door? Do you have a friend that you feel incomplete when they are not there? That was One-simus.

Notice how the gospel gave value to this man, who once was of little importance. Now he is cherished in the eyes of the Lord and Paul himself. The gospel adds value to our friends. The gospel tells us that our friends are not insignificant. The gospel gives value to what the world sees as valueless. This means the store clerk is as significant as the CEO.

THE GIFT OF A FRIEND

I used to work for a mission agency. Part of my job entailed traveling to different countries with local churches and connecting these churches to people groups that were in spiritual and physical need. One of the greatest memories I have from that time was while I was serving in Venezuela. I was prayer walking with a team through a village that neighbored a trash dump. While walking through this village, we met a mother of two children. We asked this woman, "How can we pray for you?" She responded by saying, "Pray for my family. My toddler has a stomach bug." This may seem insignificant to some, but when your children are already malnourished a simple stomach bug can quickly become a deadly thing.

After praying with this woman, she let us know that she wanted to give us a gift since we prayed for her. In this culture, not accepting a gift from someone is an insult and comes across as if you think you are better than the person. She cooked burritos from things she found in the trash dump. We ate the burritos that she gave us.

It is arguably one of the greatest gifts that I have ever received. Because of this woman's incredible love, the image of this scene is embedded into my mind. This woman may seem insignificant to some, but she changed my life and my heart. Christ comes and dies for "the least of these." The king of the universe gives up the riches of the world for those whom the world sees as having no value.

Paul now has the responsibility to train others to live in light of this reality. Living on the other side of the cross has allowed Paul to see the beauty of all types of people. Paul takes his relationship with Onesimus a step further when he appeals to Philemon saying,

> So if you consider me your partner, receive him as you would receive me. If he has wronged you at all, or owes you anything, charge that to my account. I, Paul, write this with my own hand: I will repay it—to say nothing of your owing me even your own self. Yes, brother, I want some benefit from you in the Lord. Refresh my heart in Christ (Philemon 1:17-20).

Paul in essence has said, "Whatever the cost, even if it costs me everything, I'll give it to you in hopes of keeping this dear brother. Money is of no value compared to the joy of knowing this dear brother." This sort of unity is a direct result of the gospel's transforming power. Michael Haykin, in his book, *The God Who Draws Near*, reflects on another relationship in scripture that reflects these same qualities when he says,

> For example, in 1Samuel 18:1 we read that the 'soul of Jonathan was knit to the soul of David, and Jonathan loved him as his own soul.' This reflection on the meaning of friendship bears with it ideas of strong emotional attachment and loyalty. Not surprisingly, the term 'friend' naturally became another name for believers or brothers and sisters in the Lord (see 3 John 14)."[7]

The gospel's transforming power unites the unlikely together. It places two people together that normally would not connect, and it causes a person to wonder, "How did I ever live my life without this person in it?"

AN UNCOMMON FRIENDSHIP

This sort of relationship is not common. Generally people befriend those who are like them; those who are in the same social-class as them; those who have common similarities as them. The gospel unites all types of people together for a common mission.

---

7 Michael A. G. Haykin, *The God Who Draws Near: An Introduction to Biblical Spirituality* (Darlington, England: Evangelical Press, 2007), 73.

We should treat our friends in such a way that it declares that they are of great value to us, because through the lens of the gospel we are able to see how much that person is loved by God. Sometimes loving this way is difficult, because we have been wronged many times in our relationships. In the next chapter, we will look at how the gospel changed Paul's understanding of forgiveness within relationships.

4
JOHN MARK

When you hear the name "Operation Auca," you may think that sounds like a great historic battle. You may then get images in your mind of a shirtless Rambo running out of the jungle with a bandana around his head and carrying an AR-57 with a bayonet on the end. Ok, maybe not Rambo and the AR, but you get the point. Although you may not be familiar with the name "Operation Auca," it is a famous historic event. In the 1950s, Jim Elliot, Pete Fleming, Ed McCully, Nate Saint, and Roger Youderian began plans of reaching the Huaorani people of Ecuador for the name of Christ.

The Aucas were a tribe that were known for their violence, which they performed on most outsiders. A common practice of this tribe was to spear to death their enemies. In hopes of reaching this people group, the five men mentioned earlier began flying over their village and dropping packages of supplies down from their plane. This progressed and the men began speaking Huaorani—the tribe's native tongue—phrases through a loudspeaker, which they learnt from someone who had escaped the village. The goal was to build a friendly relationship with the village people, which in time they hoped would give them an opportunity to share the gospel.

The first time the team landed their plane, they were all speared to death. The tragic death of these men made national headlines. Their story made it onto the cover of Life Magazine. This story did not end with these men's deaths.

Nate Saint's sister, Rachel, and his son, Steve, later went back to this village. They were welcomed by the people. They were able to share the gospel with the entire village. The entire village ended up coming to Christ. Steve Saint now travels the world with the man who speared his father to death and tells others about Christ.

THE DIFFICULT TASK OF FORGIVENESS

I did not grow up in the era when these events took place. I do remember when I first heard the story of these great giants of the faith. The first time I ever heard this story was from John Piper's sermon "Doing Missions When Dying is Gain." There are not many sermons that I have heard in my lifetime where the content of the sermon has stuck with me for a long period of time.

This sermon, and this story from the sermon, most certainly have stuck with me throughout the years. This story, fairly recently, was made into a major motion picture.[8] With the recent passing of Elizabeth Elliot, Jim Elliot's widow, this story once again was brought to the forefront of my mind. I tell this story not to celebrate death, but to show the power of the gospel.

This story testifies to the gospel's ability to make forgiveness possible where it may seem impossible. Because of the gospel, two men (Steve Saint and his father's killer) who have every reason to hate one another, have become friends. The Apostle Paul has a similar story of how the cross caused him to see forgiveness differently.

The next friend Paul lists in his group of friends is a man named Mark. Mark is the cousin of Barnabas. After mentioning Mark, Paul then gives an introduction to this friend saying, "Concerning whom you have received instructions—if he comes to you, welcome him." Why would the Colossians need to be told to welcome this brother?

A TIME TO DEPART WAYS

In Acts 15, we are told of story of a man named "John" who was called "Mark." John Mark was the center of the debate between Paul and Barnabas. Barnabas wanted to bring John Mark

---

8 *End of the Spear,* produced by 20th Century Fox, 2006.

along with them, and Paul did not think it would be wise to do so. This wasn't your average ordinary discussion among friends. Luke describes the dispute, saying, "And there arose a sharp disagreement, so that they separated from each other."

Do you ever get into arguments with your friends? Have you ever had a fight that ended with you both agreeing: we would be better off going our separate ways? Paul, Barnabus, and John Mark had. Our focus though need not be on the fight. Arguments and disputes will continue in this world until Christ returns. The thing which the reader should notice from this story is Paul's willingness to accept him back. Many times within our relationships when someone has wronged us or angered us, we run for the hills. We abandoned the person. We look down at our phone and see their number and we hit the "ignore" button. Paul teaches us here that the gospel demands something greater. The gospel calls for forgiveness and reconciliation.

GOD INITIATES FORGIVENESS

Throughout the Bible a motif that stands at the forefront is the fact that man is sinful, yet God in His gracious mercy reaches down and redeems him. God finds a way to accomplish this without abandoning His holiness and righteousness. This motif begins as early as Adam and Eve. Once

Adam and Eve sin, God sacrifices an animal and covers them (Gen. 3:21).

Cain sins against Abel and kills him. God then provides Cain with a mark, which is a reminder of God's judgment upon him, but also God's gracious redemption of him. No one will harm Cain because of this sin. It is similar to the cross, it is a graphic reminder of our sin and God's redemption. As the reader progresses through the Old Testament narrative he comes to Mount Sinai.

Generally, when Christians come to Mount Sinai and the Law a common misconception takes place. Christians will associate the Law with being something that is bad. The Law is not something that is bad. We think and hear things like, "Jews believed they were saved through obedience to the Law." If the Law was bad, why would the Psalmist say, "The law of the Lord is perfect refreshing the soul (Ps. 19:7)."

Furthermore, it is interesting how the Ten Commandments begin. The Ten Commandments begin with YHWH saying, "I am the Lord your God, who brought you out of the land of Egypt, out of the house of slavery." Israel had already been delivered from slavery. YHWH was already Israel's Lord whenever He gave them the Law. Israel did not need to work for redemption, because they had already been redeemed.

The Law was instruction for a redeemed people. Not only did He already redeem them, but He also made sacrifice possible to cover their sin. God, constantly throughout the Bible, sees man in his filth and God reaches down and redeems him. God makes forgiveness possible, yet not at the expense of His holiness. God is not an angry God who is just out to get you. God is a God who sees you in your sinfulness, yet is gracious to forgive and offer atonement. At the cross of Christ, God's love and justice meet. It is here we learn what it means to live Christianly. It is this event that shapes Paul's understanding of forgiveness.

LIVING IN LIGHT OF THE CROSS

Paul was forgiven of much, therefore he modeled how to forgive of much. Paul understood what it meant to forgive seventy times seven times (Matt. 18:21-22). What began as a schism ended with these brothers being restored to one another. Paul lived out being one because God himself is one (Deut. 6:4; 1 Cor. 8:6; Eph. 4:1-4). Paul tells the Colossians "to welcome this brother if he comes." Forgiveness requires us welcoming the offending party back. The Colossians likely heard about this division which took place. This, then, called for Paul to instruct them on how to respond to this brother.

Paul forgave, and he also encouraged the Colossians to do so, as well. It is as if Paul is saying, "Do not hold that transgression against this brother. Our fellowship between one another has been restored." By welcoming this brother back, Paul was able to display the character of God. He was able to display what it looks like when heaven comes down to earth and transforms a person's friendships. Are you quick to forgive when a friend has wronged you? Sometimes we justify not forgiving a person based on the egregiousness of their sin toward us.

Remember this: No matter how bad a person has wronged you, it looks very small when you look at the cross. Life on the other side of the cross calls for forgiving of much in light of the fact that we have been forgiven of much. This type of forgiveness is only possible by the work of the Spirit. What does his sort of forgiveness look like. Matt Chandler is his book, *Recovering Redemption*, describes it rather well,

> When we go to someone as a believer to seek that person's forgiveness, the gospel motivates us to not get caught up in defending ourselves or winning an argument, but to be concerned primarily with restoring peace— the way God the Father has restored peace to us through the blood of Jesus Christ.[9]

Forgiveness within our friendships is not about righting the wrong, but it is about lavishly pouring out the love of Christ, even when it is at our own expense. Maybe you have been reflecting upon your relationships while reading this and have determined that you have fallen short of this great calling. You too can be forgiven by both

---

9 Matt Chandler and Michael Snetzer, *Recovering Redemption: A Gospel-Saturated Perspective on How to Change* (Nashville, Tn: Broadman and Holman Publishing Company, 2014), 181.

God and your friends. You may think that the hour-glass is running out of sand in several of your friendships. The beauty of the gospel is that we can take the hour-glass, and turn it over, and start all over again. I can think of one particular friendship of mine where this is what we both had to do.

SLAYING ELEPHANTS AND RESTORING UNION

Time, distance, families, etc., slowly separated me from this friend. There were several things which we both became frustrated over with one another. We decided to have a "State of the Nation" address and discuss the awkward elephant in the room. This conversation required humility and love on both our parts. We forgave one another and turned the hour glass back over. We don't return to our previous faults and throw them back in one another's faces. No, we proclaim through the gospel that each one of us has been forgiven of more than we both deserve.

Do you have a John Mark type of friendship in your life? Maybe you have wronged someone and you are their John Mark. Try to initiate the process of reconciliation. It may take time. It may not be easy, but it undoubtedly will be worth it. Lets say the person does not forgive you. Was this then a lost cause? No! You were able to display the ability of the gospel to transform your heart and your life.

Once Paul and John Mark reconciled to one another, that would not be the last time you will hear about John Mark. John Mark would later write the gospel of Mark. He also would play a key role dividing the word of God in the Jerusalem Church (Acts 15). John Mark played a significant role in the church after all of this. N.T. Wright describes John Mark's transformation this way, "Mark is clearly being rehabilitated both as a worker for the gospel and as a companion of Paul."[10] Forgiveness changed the course of Paul's and John Mark's relationship. It can and will change yours as well. Take the first step. Be willing to take risks for the sake of the gospel.

---

10 N.T. Wright, *Colossians and Philemon, Tyndale New Testament Commentary Series* (Downers Grove: Il: IVP Academic, 1986), 160.

5
EPAPHRAS

When I first arrived at Bible College, I began hearing the name "Charles Spurgeon" quite frequently. I thought it was a little strange, because prior to arriving, I had never heard of his name before. I probably did hear his name before in passing but never really tied the dots together. I would enter in a classroom and I would overhear someone talking about him, his books, or his ministry. My initial reaction was, "Man I want to go hear this man preach. Spurgeon must be an incredible preacher if everyone calls him the 'Prince of Preachers.'" I began to think to myself, "Is his church near the campus?" If so, it may be worth it to travel to hear him preach.

I quickly became better acquainted with Charles Spurgeon and his writings. Throughout my collegiate career, I had the joy of studying this man's life and ministry quite extensively. Spurgeon quickly became a spiritual role model for me. You may think that is strange to have a dead role model, but as one of my former professors always said, "All my best friends are dead."[11] When you start reading about a person, and then you progress to reading their writings, that person quickly begins to feel like a close friend.

Spurgeon's life and ministry were very fascinating. One historian explains what Spurgeon's weekly routine looked like, saying,

> There were sermons to prepare weekly for his Metropolitan Tabernacle congregation (which numbered 5,311 members the time of his death). There were some 300 Sunday School teachers, with 8,000 scholars, to supervise. He had also to preside over a Pastor's College and a children's Orphanage, in addition to preparing a monthly magazine, *The Sword and the* Trowel, and other works of authorship.[12]

In addition to these things, Spurgeon found time to write over 250 hand-written letters a week. When you think about all the things that Spurgeon accomplished throughout a week, it starts to sound like he was more a machine than he was an actual person. Adding to all this, Spurgeon preached to his enormous congregation before there was even audio equipment.

---

11 This quote was given by Dr. Chad Brand

12 Iain H. Murray, *Letters of Charles Spurgeon* (Carlisle, Pa: Banner of Truth, 1992), 12.

Spurgeon once was prepping his voice for his upcoming sermon and he shouts, "Behold, the lamb of God, which takes away the sin of the world." A worker unaware of what was going to happen at the auditorium that particular day overheard Spurgeon shout this. The worker then comes under the conviction of the Holy Spirit and puts his faith in Christ. Things like this don't happen to normal people. I think this adds to the list of things which make Charles Spurgeon interesting.

This past year my wife and kids blessed me with an incredible Father's day present. My wife ordered me a sermon manuscript that was written by Charles Spurgeon. The company which my wife ordered it from was extremely busy, which delayed the delivery of my present. I remember checking the mail every day when I came home. While reading this you may be thinking that is just a Reformed version of an "icon." To be honest, I have yet to charge others a fee to come to my house and pray to it. You may think that this is rather strange, but I love history and the thought of being able to hold in my hands a handwritten document from one of my spiritual heroes seemed very cool to me.

A SPIRITUAL COACH

We all have people that we admire and long to be more like. Sometimes our aspirations to be like these heroes can be taken too far. For the most part, having a role model or a hero which you long to be more like is a healthy thing. Whether spiritual or secular we all have people like this in our lives. Maybe you work for a sales company and there is a leader that constantly stands out ahead of the pack. You slowly start taking things from his routine or his delivery and apply them to your own approach.

If you walked into your local bookstore, or even through the terminal of any airport, you will quickly realize that the majority of the shelf-space is filled with books from the "leadership" genre. Great leaders of businesses and teams often will write books to help others model their work to be more like the leader. We all have people we model our lives after in some fashion. Have you ever wondered whether or not the Apostle Paul had a spiritual role model or someone that he mentored? Did one of the most significant figures of the New Testament have someone he admired and long to be more like? Your initial reaction would be "yes, it was Jesus (1 Cor. 11:1)." That is most certainly true, but did Paul have someone he looked to in order to help him be more like Jesus? Did Paul have a young journeyman whom he shepherded? If so, who was that person and what was he like?

Toward the end of Colossians 4, Paul mentions one of his friends, a man named Epaphras. Church history tells us that Epaphras was likely the one who brought the gospel to the city of Colossae for the first time. We will see from Colossians either Epaphras was the spiritual mentor for Paul or Epaphras modeled his ministry after the Apostle Paul. Epaphras most certainly followed Paul's example as he followed Christ. I certainly imagine both men gleaned much wisdom from one another. Where do I get this idea from?

THE DISCIPLE AND THE DISCIPLER

Paul introduces Epaphras by describing him in several interesting ways. Paul begins his introduction of Epaphras by saying,

> Epaphras, who is one of you, a **servant** of Christ Jesus, greets you, always **struggling** on your behalf in his prayers, that you may stand **mature** and fully assured **in all the will of God.** 13 For I bear him witness that he has **worked hard for you** and for those in Laodicea and in Hierapolis.[13]

The first thing which Paul says about Epaphras is that he is a "servant" of the Lord. In several of the letters Paul wrote to churches, he uses this same term to describe himself (Rom. 1:1; 2 Tim. 1:3; Titus 1:1). Next, Paul says that Epaphras is "always struggling for" the Colossians in his prayers. Paul began his letter to the Colossians by saying to them,

> 28 Him we proclaim, warning everyone and teaching everyone with all wisdom, that **we**

---

13 Cf., Colossians 4:12-13 [bold and underline font I added].

may present everyone mature in Christ. **29** For this I toil, **struggling with all his energy** that he powerfully works within me.

The same phrase Paul used to describe Epaphras he used to describe himself. Paul and Epaphras "struggled" on behalf of the Colossians. Next, Paul in Colossians 4 says that the reason Epaphras devoted himself to pray for this congregation was so that they may "stand 'mature.'"

Interestingly enough, Paul in Colossians 1 describes his motivation for teaching the Colossians was so that they may be "mature in Christ." Paul said that Epaphras struggled for the Colossians so that they may be assured in "all the will of God." Once again, Paul back in Colossians 1 describes his ministry in a similar fashion, saying,

9And so, from the day we heard, we have not ceased to pray for you, asking that **you may be filled with the knowledge of his will** in all spiritual wisdom and understanding,

Paul concludes his description of Epaphras by saying that he "worked hard for you."

Paul uses similar language to describe his ministry toward the Colossians, saying he struggled with "all his energy" for them. What can we glean from the similarities between these two men? First, both Paul and Epaphras both use their friendship as a means of serving the local church. Paul's missionary journeys were marked by love and time spent with local churches. It is only natural that if he were mentoring a young man, it would be passed along to his young protégé.

Isn't it amazing how when you start to spend time with a good friend that your tastes and similarities start looking similar. I grew up in the country in a small town in Knoxville, Tn. Whenever I moved to Louisville, Kentucky, many of my friends were really big into coffee. I am not even sure that I liked coffee before I moved up to Louisville. After living nine years with some incredible believers, who happened to love good coffee, I became a huge coffee lover. I now own a great deal of coffee equipment, roast my own coffee, and honestly, I cannot see my life without it. Coffee has become a thing that I associate with places, relationships, and events in my life. It takes me back to dinner tables, desserts with friends, and rich conversations.

When you spend time with people long enough you start to look like them. This is a warning, but also a great encouragement. Paul and Epaphras were passionate about similar things. The mission of God fueled their relationship. They both desired to see God's people mature in the knowledge of His will. Epaphras may have taken Paul's command to heart: "Follow me as I follow Christ." In the end, the disciple started to look like the discipler. Do you have a mentor that is walking with you down the road of your Christian walk? Are you investing your life into other people?

THE GOAL OF GODLINESS

The goal of friendship is not simply companionship, although that is certainly a part of it. A major aspect of friendship is helping the other person mature, grow, and fulfill their life's intended purpose—becoming more like Christ. Maybe you do not have any relationships like this to which you can point. Let me challenge you, start forming relationships that look like this with your friends. Walk with them through maturity and growth. Jesus often turned away the crowds to devote himself to the twelve.

Later on, he would send out the twelve to reach the multitudes. You will not find a better picture of a mentor type of friendship/relationship than that. Jesus demonstrates friendship that is centered on love, yet focused on spiritual maturity and mission. Are you an Epaphras? Encourage and love your mentor. Build this person up. Thank the Lord for blessing you with someone like him or her.

However, you too are called to be a Paul. Take a risk and starting investing your life into someone. You don't need to have a system in place to accomplish this. Simply make your aim to help your friends look more like Jesus on a regular basis.

6
LUKE

It was the summer of my eighth grade year. I had spent the summer with one of my best friends rotating between his house and mine. We were inseparable that summer. One weekend that summer, we decided to visit his aunt's house to go fishing and ride 4-wheelers. At the time, I didn't meet the stereotypical mold of a Southerner, because that weekend would be my first time riding a 4-wheeler.

The weekend began with us spending a day riding the trials back in the woods. At one point in the day, I was riding with my friend's aunt and I was holding on to the cargo rack on the back of the 4-wheeler. While driving down a hill, we hit a large bump that caused the 4-wheeler to go several feet off the ground before it returned to the ground with a strong bounce. This bounce produced enough force to break both of my arms at the same time. What began as a day filled with fun and entertainment ended rather tragically. My friend's parents rushed me to the ER in order for a doctor to operate on my broken arms. I desperately needed a physician to care for me during this time.

THE TWO PHYSICIANS

Everyone at some point in time has had a need for a physician. Maybe you haven't broken a bone, but you have certainly been to a physician for a check-up or possibly even to receive your regulated vaccinations. No matter your age or your physical fitness, we all need a physician at some point in time for our health needs. Now let's look at another related scenario.

I can recall two situations in my life that were both very emotionally draining and spiritually challenging times in my life. It was through a word spoken by a mentor/friend of mine that I found comfort and hope during this difficult time. This friend acted as a spiritual physician for my soul. He cut out the painful cancer and restored life to my soul.

The Puritans used to call people like this "physicians of the soul." Similar to a doctor who has cared for our physical health, many of us have experienced a "spiritual physician" who has cared for something far more significant, he/she has cared for our souls. Think back to a time where you may have been struggling with something, lost hope, or were discouraged. Like

Humpty Dumpty, you may have fallen off the wall and you feel like your life has been shattered into pieces. A "spiritual physician" will climb down the wall and slowly, with the gospel, help put you back together piece by piece. One place in scripture where this destruction and rebuilding process can be seen the clearest is in the book of Isaiah.

THE COMING COMFORTER

The book of Isaiah begins by the Lord revealing how Israel has sinned against Him. Isaiah is then commissioned to go and proclaim the coming judgment upon Israel. Judgment was certain, and the people would not repent. God did not leave His people there without hope. Similar to how God gave Adam and Eve hope shortly after the Fall. He once again demonstrates His great love and mercy to His people. The way in which Israel was to know that God had not abandoned them in the midst of their judgment was going to be the birth of a child.

Isaiah describes this child saying he shall be called, "Wonderful counselor, Mighty God, Everlasting Father, and Prince of peace (Isaiah 9:7)." Isaiah goes on to describe this child as the one who would bring Edenic restoration (Isaiah 11; 35; 53:1). Through this child, the lion would lie down with the lamb, and the child next to the den of vipers. The harmony that was lost because of the Fall will be restored through this child. It is interesting that the son of Isaiah 7 and 9 will be one who brings "peace," and furthermore, he is described as a "wonderful counselor."

Matthew picks up these passages and says that they were typologically fulfilled in Christ. Jesus then lives the life in which Israel could not live by perfectly obeying the Father. Through his death, reconciliation is then accomplished. Jesus, then, promises to send the Holy Spirit after his departure, and he uses similar language to describe the Spirit. Jesus calls the Holy Spirit the "comforter" in John 14:26. The Holy Spirit is called the "advocate," one which pleads on your behalf in John 15:26.

Finally, the Holy Spirit is called the "Spirit of Truth" in John 16:13. The role of the Spirit is to guide a believer to truth. Jesus sends the Spirit to comfort those who were in Christ. When the Spirit indwells a believer, not only does He comfort that person, but he also produces within that person a heart to reflect these same characteristics to others. A "spiritual physician" is one who "comforts" other believers during their time of need. A "spiritual physician" is the type of person who sees a brother or sister who may be down or broken and he preaches "truth" into their lives. Does an image of a friend come to mind when you hear about these qualities? Paul had a friend like this. Paul had a friend who was both a physician of his health and spiritual physician of his soul.

A PHYSICIAN FOR HIS HEALTH

Paul introduces Luke, another one of his dear friends, in Colossians 4:14. Paul begins by describing Luke as a "beloved physician." Luke traveled around with Paul and cared for him during his many persecutions. In 2 Corinthians 11, Paul describes his many persecutions, and likely the reason for needing a traveling physician when he said,

> ...with far greater labors, far more imprisonments, with countless beatings, and often near death. Five times I received at the hands of the Jews the forty lashes less one. Three times I was beaten with rods. Once I was stoned. Three times I was shipwrecked; a night and a day I was adrift at sea; on frequent journeys, in danger from rivers, danger from robbers, danger from my own people, danger from Gentiles, danger in the city, danger in the wilderness, danger at sea, danger from false brothers; in toil and hardship, through many a sleepless night, in hunger and thirst, often without food, in cold and exposure (2 Cor. 11).

In the midst of these persecutions Paul said that Luke was by his side during these difficult times (2 Tim. 4:11; Philemon 1:23). Luke was a physician for his health, but also a spiritual physician as well. When we think of Luke, we often do not think of him simply as a physician. When we think of Luke, we think of Luke the writer of the Gospel of Luke and Acts.

A PHYSICIAN FOR HIS SOUL

Luke begins his gospel by saying he wrote the gospel for the certainty of Theophilus' faith. We generally equate Paul as being the theological giant of his friends. Darrell Bock, in his commentary on the Gospel of Luke, points out this interesting point, "Luke as an author was the largest contributor to the New Testament, if one counts verses (Luke wrote 2,157 verses [Luke + Acts]; Paul wrote 2032 verses."[14] Ironically, Luke contributes to a larger portion of the New Testament. Luke was a man who was both concerned with a believer's physical health and their spiritual health. Luke was a man who was concerned with ministering to a person's entire being. Luke was the type of friend that would stitch up your battle wounds and then spiritually help you fix your eyes back on the mission.

We all need friends who care for us when we are down. When a person is on their deathbed, nothing is more comforting than having a spiritual physician there caring for your soul. When a friend gets cancer they need someone to physically help them, but also someone who will point them to Christ and remind them that their suffering is not in vain. People need someone to point

---

14 Darrell L. Bock, *Luke, NAC* (Grand Rapids, Mi: Zondervan 1998), 8.

them to Christ to help them "count it as joy" when they face various trials.

Trials were not meant to be suffered alone. The way in which the Spirit displays Himself in our relationships is by giving us a heart to comfort one another. Are you comforting your friends while they are down or suffering? Are you leading your friends into truth, even when you know they may not want to hear it? Make it a goal to start developing, or practicing, these spiritual habits in your friendships. Great friendships have to start somewhere. Every runner who has ever won a marathon has only done so by taking the first step. Sometimes that step is the hardest, but the end-prize far outweighs the struggle.

7
DEMAS

One of my favorite times of the year is the arrival of fall. Words cannot accurately express the beauty of seeing all the colors that mark the tree lines along the interstates down South. Fall brings with it a unique special smell to the air. There is something special about sitting out on your front porch and hearing drum cadences from local high school marching bands as they prep for the upcoming football season.

Fall brings with it a sea of sporting paraphernalia, representing each town's local university. During the fall, the drive home takes longer than normal because you must avoid children in the streets. Children run throughout the streets imagining that they are the next great NFL star throwing a touchdown pass to one of their neighborhood friends. There are pumpkins, pumpkin patches, pumpkin pie, pumpkin spice lattes, corn mazes, hay rides, and the list could go on. It is one of those lists in life that honestly should end with a comma rather than a period. The only sad thing about fall is its length. It is painful when the seasons transition from fall to winter.

The beautiful colors transition into dead leaves on the ground. The echoes of cheerful children's voices running through the street slowly transition into the sound of hallowing winter wind down deserted streets. As winter slowly takes over, you feel as if you lost something valuable to you. You feel as if you have been robbed. You then begin to pray that the thing you cherished would return soon.

Maybe you do not have the same feelings about fall that I do. Can you think of something else dear to you that you have lost, yet you long for it to come back? We all have a similar scenario of losing something valuable and longing to have it returned. The metal detector industry exists and thrives based upon this reality. Organizations keep a "lost and found" because they know that sometimes people lose something that is valuable to them and that they will return in hopes of getting it back. The Apostle Paul was no different than the rest of us. He once lost something or someone dear to him. Colossians 4 tells us the story of a friend that got away.

FROM CO-LABORER TO HEART-BREAKER

While Paul was traveling on his missionary journeys, a man named Demas accompanied him.

FRIENDSHIP REDEEMED

Paul described Demas in his letter to Philemon as a "co-laborer." While Paul was saying his good-byes in his letter to the Colossians he let them know that "Demas greets them." Demas was not the type of guy who met Paul once and then named-dropped him every so often in order to move up the corporate ladder. Demas was very involved in the life and ministry of Paul.

From the frequency of their travels, and Paul's multiple citations of him, he seemed to be a good friend and ministry partner to Paul. What happened then that caused their relationship to go awry? Paul actually tells the story of the tragic turning point in their relationship. Paul after being arrested was abandoned by Demas. Paul was abandoned during a time of need. Paul describes this abandonment by saying,

> For Demas, having loved this present world, has deserted me and gone to Thessalonica; Crescens has gone to Galatia, Titus to Dalmatia (2 Tim. 4:10).

When life got hard, Demas abandoned Paul and left him all alone. Can you recall a time in your life when things got really difficult and someone close to you abandoned you. Trusting in this type of person is analogous to trusting the Proverbs 25:19 man. Proverbs 25:19 makes a warning about this type of person by saying, "trusting in a treacherous man in time of trouble is like a bad tooth or a foot that slips." Sam Storms is very helpful with connecting the two when he says,

DEMAS

Nothing hurts quite like the disloyalty and betrayal of someone trusted. It's like a decaying, rotten tooth and a palsied, disjointed foot. Not only are they functionally useless (for chewing and walking), they hurt! For some of you, no doubt, your experience with this sort of person has made you hesitant to trust another. Perhaps you've closed your heart to starting new friendships or found yourself keeping folk at arm's length. But Paul didn't let the betrayal and abandonment of Demas and others scare him off or sour him to friendship altogether.[15]

Thinking back now on Paul's friend John Mark. In Paul's list here of his friends, he has two friends now that have abandoned him. How can you tell whether one of your friends is going to be a John Mark (a friend that leaves and comes back) or a Demas (a friend that leaves you and never returns)? You can't! So, should we shut the door on any friendship in fear that they may abandon us or hurt us? No! Paul models for us how living on the other side of the cross calls for believers to take risks with others. Sometimes you are going to get hurt.

---

15 Sam Storms, *The Hope of Glory: 100 Devotions on Colossians* (Wheaton, IL: Crossway Publishing Company, 2007), 343.

A RISK WORTH TAKING

One of the most common reasons I hear when I meet people who have left the church is that they left because someone hurt them. This reasoning is true for friendships as well. A person gets hurt and he allows that pain to be an excuse to shut everyone else out of his or her life. Paul models a radical alternate response for us when these situations arise. Paul demonstrates how the gospel demands that we take risks on others.

Paul's life and ministry are a testimony to others willing to take a risk on him. Paul went from killing Christians to being one. I imagine that Christians were not lining up to have him over for dinner shortly after his conversion. Rather than being safe, take risks for the sake of the gospel. Rather than leaving the church because you have been hurt, stay and be an agent of change. You may get hurt along the way, but the joy of seeing others transformed will far outweigh any pain that you may receive. You will experience a Demas or two along the way, but keep your eyes on the cross and be willing to take risks with others. Be prepared to accept the wayward friend back, but also be prepared to separate when necessary. Paul separated from both John Mark and Demas when their friendships slowed down advancing the kingdom of God. In our last chapter, we will look at why it is important to surround yourself with friends that are passionate about kingdom advancement.

8
KINGDOM ADVANCING FRIENDSHIPS

"He who walks with wise men will be wise."
Proverbs 13:20

An old adage says that "a man is known by the company he keeps." Growing up, I was always warned to choose my friends wisely. My mom warned me that my friends could be the thing that kept me out of trouble or in it. Now that I have become a parent, I too am nervous for my children and the friends whom they will select. Part of a parent's responsibility is to weed out potential bad friends, but a parent can never know for certainty.

Generally, when a child goes wayward, his/her parents will say, "Well he just got caught up in the wrong crowd." A constant fear of any parent is that their child will join that wrong crowd and continue on a downward spiral. The people who you surround yourself with will inevitably have an impact upon your life.

A little over ten years ago, one of my best friends talked me into moving away from home and attending Bible College with him. You may think that at a Bible College everyone is serious about their studies, but that is not always the case. Do not hear me as saying that I question the hearts or motives of those attending these schools. What I am saying is that there was a certain crowd within my school that everyone knew if you were around them, you were going to be thrown into a deep or serious conversation about the bible.

When I arrived at Bible College my best friend had already befriended other friends who took the bible seriously. My friend took me, an immature young college kid, and threw me right into the heart of this group. Initially it wasn't that I could not follow the conversations these men were having, it was that I didn't even know the words they were using. The passion and zeal these men displayed when discussing these topics sent me off on a research project to be able to keep up with their conversations. Prior to this, my only research revolved around determining who my first 5 picks were going to be in the upcoming fantasy football draft. Because of these men, my desires changed.

I once hated reading, but now it has become a love of mine. Because of these men, I look at life completely different. These men caused me to reinterpret all of reality. That which was simple and assumed on my part was radically challenged. I went to Bible College as one person, but left a completely different person. I say all this to tell you that the people with whom you surround yourself have a far greater influence on you than you know. Paul in Colossians 4 testifies to the importance of surrounding yourself with kingdom-minded men.

THE MEN THAT MADE PAUL

Paul surrounded himself with faithful and trusting men. The men in Colossians 4 were more than just coworkers of Paul. These men were loved in his eyes. These co-workers in ministry were transformed into Paul's friends. These men were spiritual physicians, who motivated one another toward kingdom advancement. All too often, people simply surround themselves with people who are like-minded. You may meet a person and think this person likes sports and I like sports, so you end up becoming friends.

Paul shows us how the gospel can make two people who are nothing at all alike and make them the best of friends. Paul challenges us to take risks on people even when they are not like us. Paul's friends were made up of a pretty diverse group of individuals—a former slave, a doctor, both Jews and Gentiles, etc. If you only have friends who are like you, you will never be challenged to be something more or something different. If all your friends are similar, you will never mature past who you are currently.

Paul models how to love others when they have wronged you. People in general are quick to turn their backs on those who have wronged them. Paul displays a forgiveness that is only possible through the Holy Spirit. It is a forgiveness that was displayed on the cross when the God of the universe gave up his life when everyone had wronged him. Paul models how to let friends go when they hinder the advancement of the gospel, but he also models how to welcome them back whenever they have returned. Paul sets before the Colossians a band of brothers that were knitted together by and for the gospel.

May your friendships be transformed by the gospel through the power of the Spirit.

ABOUT THE AUTHOR

Adam Holland resides in Knoxville, TN with his wife, Katelyn, and their children—Emma Kate and Isaiah. He graduated from Boyce College (B.A.) and the Southern Baptist Theological Seminary (M.Div.). He frequently writes articles and reviews for several different online, newspaper, and magazine publications.

Purchase at TheVeritasNetwork.org

When Jesus saves us, everything changes. If we understand this, then our practice of dating, sex, and marriage simply cannot stay the same. The logic is pretty clear. Jesus saves us. Jesus changes us. Jesus changes how we view and practice things. Dating is one of those things. Sex is one of those things. Marriage is one of those things. Let's begin a conversation about how Jesus calls us to... Date Different.

CPSIA information can be obtained
at www.ICGtesting.com
Printed in the USA
LVHW081521311218
602287LV00020B/1505/P

9 780692 541586